Herman Hertzberger
Strukturalismus
Structuralism

HIRMER

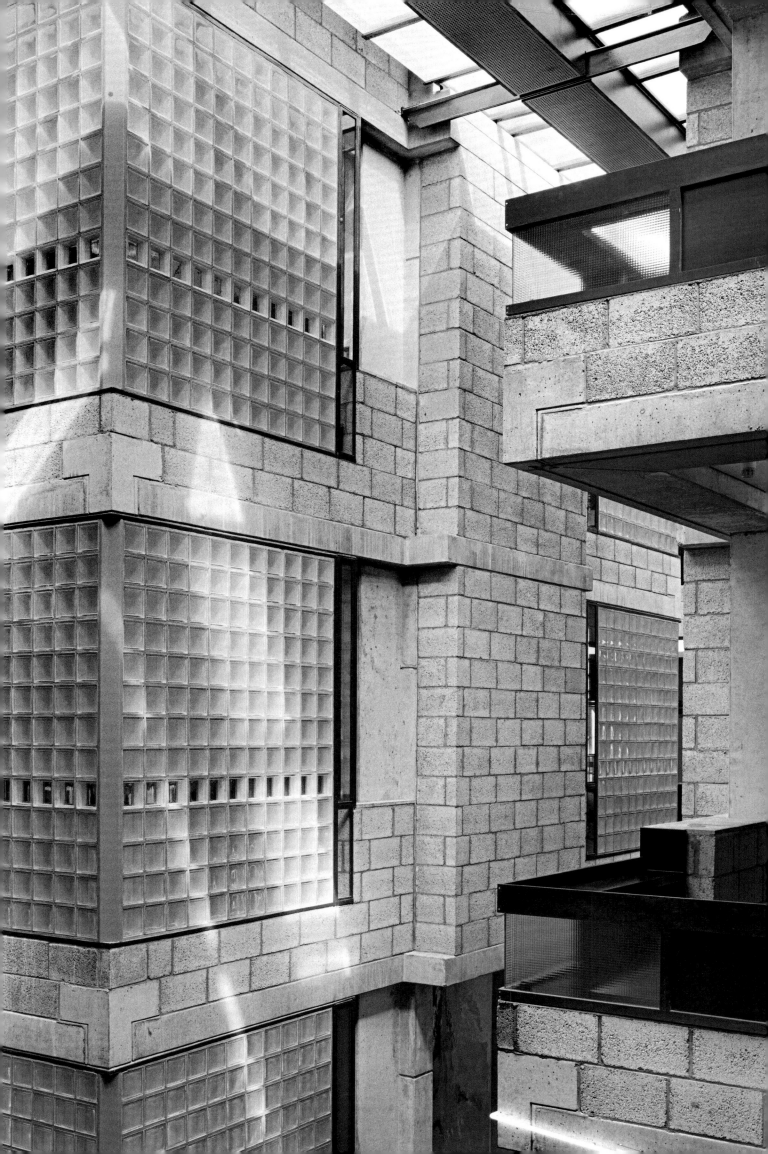

Everything in architecture, good or bad, in which the constructive aspect occupies a visually prominent position, and which has to do with repetition of prefabricated components with grids or frames, is labeled structuralism. Structuralism denoted, initially, a way of thinking originating form cultural anthropology, which rose to prominence in Paris during the sixties and which, especially in the form developed by Claude Lévi-Strauss, exerted a strong influence on the various social sciences.

Language is structure par excellence, a structure that, in principle, contains the possibilities to express everything that can be communicated verbally. It is indeed a prerequisite for the ability to think. For an idea can only be said to exist in so far as it permits formulation in words.

In the philosophy of structuralism this idea is extended to encompass an image of man whose possibilities are constant and fixed, like a pack of cards with which you can play different games depending on the way they have been dealt.

Broadly speaking, "structure" stands for the collective, general, objective. One could also speak of structure in connection with a building or an urban plan: a large form which, changing little or not at all, is suitable and adequate for accommodating different situations because it offers fresh opportunities time and again for new uses.

Herman Hertzberger

Inhalt/Contents

7 Herman Hertzberger
Strukturalismus als sozialer Auftrag
Structuralism as Social Contract

12 Verwaltungsgebäude/Headquarters
Centraal Beheer, Apeldoorn

28 Musikzentrum/Music Center Vredenburg,
Utrecht

40 Apollo-Schulen/The Apollo Schools, Amsterdam

58 Schule/School De Evenaar, Amsterdam

68 Sozial- und Arbeitsministerium/Ministry of Social
Affairs and Employment, Den Haag/The Hague

78 Herman Hertzberger
Biographie/Biography

80 Impressum/Imprint

Herman Hertzberger
Strukturalismus
Structuralism

Fotografie/Photography
Klaus Kinold

Text
Wolfgang Jean Stock

Altenheim De Overloop
Almere-Haven, 1980–1984

Nursing Home De Overloop
Almere-Haven, 1980–1984

Herman Hertzberger
Strukturalismus als sozialer Auftrag

Im Jahr 1959 trat eine Gruppe niederländischer Architekten auf die internationale Bühne. Das sechs Jahre zuvor gegründete Team X nutzte den 11. Kongress der bis dahin führenden CIAM (Congrès Internationaux d'Architecture Moderne) in Otterlo für harte Kritik an der schematisch gewordenen Nachkriegsmoderne. Die jungen Niederländer vertraten eine konträre Auffassung, die später als ‚Strukturalismus' bezeichnet wurde, und erklärten die CIAM für beendet.

Wortführer des Team X war Aldo van Eyck (1918–1999), der sich schon früher gegen den Rationalismus in der modernen Architektur ausgesprochen hatte, weil dieser das Verhältnis zwischen Funktion und Raum statisch bestimme. Vielmehr komme es darauf an, den Nutzern von Gebäuden einen flexiblen Rahmen zu liefern, der individuelle Aktivitäten zulassen und fördern könne. Van Eyck ging von einem archetypischen Verhalten des Menschen aus, für das der Architekt entsprechende Strukturen finden müsse. Weil er von ‚Archeformen' in der Architektur überzeugt war, die sich im Lauf der Geschichte nur wandeln würden, gab es eine Nähe zu Ethnologen wie Claude Lévi-Strauss, der bei ‚primitiven' Völkern einen strukturalen Zusammenhang zwischen Bauformen und sozialem Leben festgestellt hatte. Van Eyck und seine Mitstreiter befanden sich damit im Widerspruch zu den Dogmen der CIAM und deren Wortführer Sigfried Giedion. Dessen damals einflussreiche Raum-Zeit-Konzeption mit einem universalen Anspruch[1] lehnte van Eyck in Otterlo entschieden ab: „Was Raum und Zeit auch immer bedeuten – Ort und Geschehen bedeuten mehr, denn in der Vorstellung des Menschen erscheint der Raum als Ort und die Zeit als Geschehnis."[2]

Van Eycks wichtigster Nachfolger und schließlich der Hauptvertreter des niederländischen Strukturalismus wurde der 1932 geborene Herman Hertzberger. Internationale Anerkennung erhielt er durch seine zwischen 1968 und 1990 ausgeführten Bürogebäude, Schulen, Altenheime und Wohnanlagen. Zu ihrem besonderen Charakter trug bei, dass er neben Sichtbeton und Glas vor allem das ‚arme' und zugleich markante Baumaterial Betonstein verwendete – das helle Sichtmauerwerk mit seinem feinen Fugennetz strahlt eine calvinistische Poesie aus.

Herman Hertzberger
Structuralism as Social Contract

In 1959 a group of Dutch architects appeared on the international stage. At the 11th congress in Otterlo of the up-to-then dominant CIAM (Congrès Internationaux d'Architecture Moderne), Team X, founded six years before, subjected schematic postwar Modernism to harsh criticism. The young Dutchmen championed another style, later known as "Structuralism," and declared CIAM defunct.

The spokesman for Team X was Aldo van Eyck (1918–1999), who had already criticized rationalism in modern architecture earlier, because it treated the relationship between function and space as static. Instead, a building's occupants were to be provided with options, with flexible spaces that allowed for and promoted different activities. Van Eyck focused on archetypical human behavior, for which the architect needed to find appropriate structures. Because he was convinced of "archeforms" in architecture that merely changed over the course of history, he was not unlike the ethnologist Claude Lévi-Strauss, who had identified a structural relationship between building forms and social life in "primitive" peoples. Van Eyck and his comrades-in-arms thus found themselves in opposition to the dogmas of CIAM and its spokesman Sigfried Giedion. In Otterlo Van Eyck roundly rejected Giedion's space-time concept with its claim to universality,[1] which was influential at the time: "Whatever space and time may mean—location and incident mean more, for in the human imagination space appears as location and time as incident."[2]

Van Eyck's most important successor and finally the main representative of Dutch structuralism was Herman Hertzberger, born in 1932. He attained international recognition with his office buildings, schools, nursing homes, and housing complexes constructed between 1968 and 1990. Part of their special character was the fact that in addition to exposed concrete and glass he made prominent use of concrete blocks, a "humble" yet striking building material whose light-colored, visible masonry with its delicate network of joints radiates a kind of Calvinist poetry.

Architektur für gemeinschaftliches Leben. Links oben ein Treppenhaus, das als vertikaler Begegnungsraum gestaltet ist, in der Berliner Wohnanlage LiMa aus dem Jahr 1986. Die anderen Fotos zeigen den Umgang von Schülerinnen mit den 1983 fertig gestellten Apollo-Schulen in Amsterdam.

Architecture for a common life. Upper left: A stairwell designed as a vertical meeting place in Berlin's LiMa housing development from 1986. The other photographs show pupils using the Apollo Schools in Amsterdam, completed in 1983.

Bei Hertzberger umfasst der Begriff ‚Struktur' beide Seiten von Architektur: Zum einen bezieht er sich auf die Konstruktion des Gebäudes, zum anderen auf seine Raumgliederung. Leitbild ist jeweils eine möglichst große Anpassungsfähigkeit an wechselnde menschliche Bedürfnisse. Herman van Bergeijk, der die maßgebliche Monografie über Hertzberger geschrieben hat, würdigt ihn als eine epochale Gestalt: „Mehr als jeder Architekt seiner Generation hat sich Hertzberger drei Themen verschrieben, die seine Arbeit von Anfang an bestimmten: Form, Funktion und Freiheit. (…) Hertzberger ist in den Niederlanden der führende Vertreter der Generation junger Nachkriegsarchitekten, einer Generation, die aus dem Ungewissen heraus an der Praxis und dogmatischen Gewissheit der (…) Nachkriegsarchitektur scharfe Kritik übte."[3] Bei einer internationalen Konferenz Ende 2009 in München, auf der unter Anwesenheit von Hertzberger an die Leistungen des Strukturalismus erinnert wurde, gab Herman van Bergeijk einen erhellenden Überblick über Ursprünge, Ausbreitung und Rezeption dieser Strömung. Dabei wies er nicht nur darauf hin, dass sich niederländische Wissenschaftler bereits vor Lévi-Strauss „mit primitiven Gesellschaften unter einem strukturalistischen Blickwinkel" beschäftigt hätten, sondern hob auch die Verdienste von Arnulf Lüchinger hervor, der durch seine Aufsätze und Bücher den Strukturalismus erst zu einem Begriff gemacht habe.[4]

Lüchinger brachte den Begriff früh in die internationale Diskussion. 1974 bewertete er in der renommierten Zeitschrift ‚Bauen + Wohnen' den Strukturalismus sogar als ‚Symbol der Demokratisierung'.[5] Das entsprach genau der sozialen Haltung von Hertzberger, der damals proklamierte: „Heute kann Architektur nur Sinn haben, wenn sie nachweisbar einen Beitrag zur Verbesserung der Bedingungen und Lebensumstände von Menschen liefert."[6]

For Hertzberger the notion of "structure" embraces both aspects of architecture. For one it refers to a building's construction, for another its spatial arrangement. In each case his aim was to provide the greatest possible adaptability to changing human requirements. Herman van Bergeijk, who wrote the authoritative monograph on Hertzberger, recognized him as an epochal figure: "More than any other architect of his generation Hertzberger has committed himself to three qualities that have defined his work from the beginning: form, function, and freedom. . . . Hertzberger is the leading representative of the generation of young postwar architects in the Netherlands, a generation that out of uncertainty exercised sharp criticism of the practice and dogmatic certainty of . . . postwar architecture."[3] At an international conference in Munich in late 2009, Van Bergeijk recalled in Hertzberger's presence the achievements of structuralism, providing an informative overview of the movement's origins, spread, and reception. In it he not only pointed out that even before Lévi-Strauss Dutch scholars had dealt "with primitive societies from a structuralist point of view," but also gave particular credit to Arnulf Lüchinger, who with his books and essays had made structuralism a recognized concept.[4]

Lüchinger introduced the concept into international discourse early on. In 1974, in the respected journal 'Bauen + Wohnen', he even judged structuralism to be a "symbol of democratization."[5] This was precisely in line with Hertzberger's social stance, who at that time proclaimed: "Architecture makes sense today only if it verifiably contributes to peoples' improved situations and living conditions."[6]

---

1 Sigfried Giedion: Raum, Zeit, Architektur. Die Entstehung einer neuen Tradition, Zürich und/and München 1976.
2 Zitiert in/quoted in Winfried Nerdinger: Baumschlager–Eberle 2002–2007. Architektur, Menschen und Ressourcen, Wien/Vienna 2007, S./p. 6.
3 Herman van Bergeijk: Herman Hertzberger, Basel • Boston • Berlin 1997, S./p. 7. Fortan zitiert als/cited below as Bergeijk: Hertzberger.
4 Herman van Bergeijk: Driving Forces behind Dutch Structuralism, in: Tomáš Valena mit/with Tom Avermaete und/and Georg Vrachliotis (Hg./eds.): Structuralism Reloaded. Rule-Based Design in Architecture and Urbanism, Stuttgart und/and London 2011, S./pp. 110-115.
5 Arnulf Lüchinger: Strukturalismus – Architektur als Symbol der Demokratisierung, in: Bauen + Wohnen, 1974, Heft/issue 5, S./pp. 209-212.
6 Herman Hertzberger: Das Gebäude als Instrument der Bewohner, in: Ebda./ibid., S./p. 211.

Schule De Evenaar
Amsterdam, 1984–1986

De Evenaar School
Amsterdam, 1984–1986

Blick über die Bahnlinie auf die Struktur der Baukörper.

View across the rail line of the building's structure.

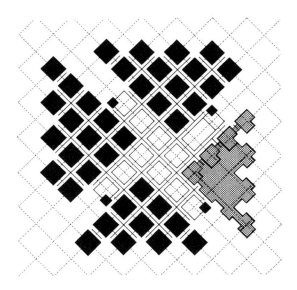

**Verwaltungsgebäude Centraal Beheer
Apeldoorn, 1968–1972**

Die neue Hauptverwaltung der Versicherungsgesellschaft Centraal Beheer in der kleinen Großstadt Apeldoorn war das Gebäude, mit dem Herman Hertzberger Anfang der 1970er Jahre international bekannt wurde. Es ist eines seiner Hauptwerke und gilt als ein herausragendes Zeugnis der zeitgenössischen Architektur. Herman van Bergeijk nennt es sogar „das einzige ‚Meisterwerk' der niederländischen Architektur der siebziger Jahre."[7]

Völlig neuartig bei einem großen Bürogebäude für 1.000 Beschäftigte waren seine Gestalt als hoch verdichteter Flachbau und der Verzicht auf Hierarchie und Repräsentation in der Raumbildung, vor allem aber die Innenzonen durch die dramatische Lichtführung und den Wechsel von Enge und Weite. Der zu seinem Zentrum hin ansteigende Komplex aus quadratischen, eng vernetzten Baukörpern, von Hertzberger als „eine Art Ansiedlung" charakterisiert, liegt isoliert zwischen mehrspurigen Straßen und einer Eisenbahnlinie. Diese Situation hätte sich gebessert, wäre ein ursprünglich geplanter Bahnhof mit anschließender Ladenzeile durch den Komplex gebaut worden. Die nebenstehende Strukturzeichnung zeigt den zellenartigen Aufbau in vier Quadranten. Die Gruppen der schwarz angelegten Büroeinheiten und der niedrigere Ostteil mit Dachterrassen werden durch einen gemeinschaftlichen Bereich miteinander verzahnt, der mit Passagen und platzartigen Erweiterungen das Bauwerk in Form eines Windmühlenflügels durchzieht. An seinen Enden liegen die vier Eingänge mit jeweils einem Besucherempfang – den bei einem solchen Bürogebäude üblichen Haupteingang gibt es nicht.

Büroinseln und Lufträume
Ausgangspunkt der Planung war die Überlegung, wie sich ein Gebäude, in dem die Beschäftigten die Hälfte ihrer bewusst erlebten Zeit verbringen, ‚wohnlich' gestalten lässt. Hertzbergers Biograf Wessel Reinink schreibt dazu: „Aus diesem Gedanken heraus wurde nach einer Form gesucht, die den Mitarbeitern die Möglichkeit bietet, sich einen eigenen Platz zu schaffen, wo sie sich zu Hause fühlen können, sowohl als Einzelner als auch in der Gruppe. In der gewählten Form wurde versucht, die Vorteile eines Großraumbüros mit denen separater

**Centraal Beheer Headquarters
Apeldoorn, 1968–1972**

The new headquarters for the Centraal Beheer insurance company in the small big town Apeldoorn was the building that made Herman Hertzberger internationally famous in the early 1970s. It is one of his major works and considered an outstanding example of contemporary architecture. Herman van Bergeijk even called it "the sole 'masterpiece' of Dutch architecture from the 1970s."[7]

Altogether novel in a large office building for 1,000 employees were its form, a highly compact, relatively flat structure, and its absence of hierarchy and ostentation in its range of spaces, above all the dramatic play of light in its interiors, with their alternating intimacy and expansiveness. The collection of square, closely linked structures rising toward the center—Hertzberger described it as "a kind of settlement"—stands isolated between four-lane streets and a railway line. This situation would have been improved if, as originally planned, a train station had been built through the complex with an adjacent row of shops. The drawing on the left shows the cellular structure in four quadrants. The groups of black office units and the lower east section with roof terraces are tied together by a common area extending through the complex, like the vanes of a windmill in shape, with passages and plaza-like spaces. At the ends are the four entrances, each with a reception area; there is no main entrance of the kind expected in such an office building.

Office Islands and Air Spaces
Crucial to the planning of the structure was how to make a building "homelike" in which employees spend half their waking lives. Hertzberger's biographer Wessel Reinink writes: "This led to a search for forms that gave employees the chance to create a space for themselves, where they can feel at home, both as solitary workers and within the group. In the design selected there was an attempt to combine the advantages of a large, open office with those of separate rooms."[8] The solution featured interlinked, flexible "office islands," each with four corner spaces measuring 3 × 3 meters. Toward the outside these corner spaces are set apart by walls of glass brick, toward the inside separated and at the same time tied together by full-height air spaces lit from above. The office

Zimmer zu kombinieren."[8] Die Lösung bestand in der Verflechtung von flexibel nutzbaren ‚Büroinseln' mit jeweils vier Eckzonen in einem Modul von 3 × 3 Metern. Nach außen hin sind die Eckzonen voll verglast, zum Inneren hin sind sie durch gebäudehohe, von oben belichtete Lufträume getrennt und zugleich verbunden. Horizontal erschlossen werden die Büroinseln durch ein regelmäßiges Wegenetz mit verglasten Brücken in den Lufträumen. Arnulf Lüchinger hat diese Konzeption als neuartige ‚Bürolandschaft' begrüßt: „Im Gegensatz zum bekannten Bürogroßraum kommt hier eine neue Dimension hinzu. Durch den Vertikalkontakt hat man das Gefühl, zur ganzen Gemeinschaft zu gehören. Die Öffnungen zwischen den einzelnen Arbeitsinseln verhindern das Dichtwachsen des Betriebs. Der Raum kann nicht ersticken, und auftretender Lärm wird genügend gedämpft. Es fällt mehr Licht ins Innere als beim traditionellen Großraum, womit der Kontakt zur Außenwelt gewährleistet ist."[9]

islands are reached horizontally by a regular network of walkways with glazed bridges in the air spaces. Arnulf Lüchinger welcomed this concept as an innovative "office landscape": "Here, in contrast to the familiar open office space, a new dimension has been added. Thanks to the vertical contact one has the feeling of being part of the whole community. The openings between the individual islands prevent the organization from becoming crowded. The space cannot become stifling and any noise is adequately muted. More light falls into the interior than into a traditional large space, providing contact with the outside world."[9]

7 Bergeijk: Hertzberger, S./p. 14.
8 Wessel Reinink: Herman Hertzberger, mit Fotografien von/*with photographs by* Klaus Kinold, Berlin 1991, S./p. 12. Fortan zitiert als/*cited below as* Reinink: Hertzberger.
9 Arnulf Lüchinger, siehe Anm./*see note* 5, S./p. 210.

Der Blick in einen Luftraum zwischen den Büroinseln zeigt die harmonische Verbindung der Baustoffe Betonstein, Stahl und Glas. Durch verglaste Dachflächen fällt das Licht in die Tiefe des Gebäudes.

A view into an air space between the office islands shows the harmonious combination of the building materials of concrete blocks, steel, and glass. Light falls into the building's depth through skylights.

Flexibilität durch Baukasten

Herman Hertzberger hat die Konstruktion als ‚Baukasten' bezeichnet, weshalb sich das Gebäude ohne großen Aufwand verändern lässt: „Ein Bürogebäude zu entwerfen, mag im Prinzip einfach sein, doch gerade die erforderliche Anpassungsfähigkeit war bei diesem Auftrag das Entscheidende. Ständige Veränderungen in der Organisation erfordern eine häufige Anpassung an die Größe der jeweiligen Abteilungen. Der Bau muss all diese internen Kräfte aufnehmen und dabei selbst als Ganzes in allen Beziehungen und zu jeder Zeit funktionieren können. (...) Als geordneter räumlicher Komplex entworfen, besteht der Bau aus einer Grundstruktur, die einen im Wesentlichen festgelegten, permanenten Kern darstellt, und einer variablen, interpretierbaren Ergänzungszone."[10] Deshalb wurde das tragende Skelett des Gebäudes mit vorgefertigten Betonelementen auf einem Stützenraster errichtet. Als prägendes Material wirken außen wie innen die hellen Betonsteine. Das gliedernde Sichtmauerwerk gibt zusammen mit den Bauteilen aus Sichtbeton, Stahl und Glas den Räumen eine freundliche, anregende Atmosphäre.

Flexibility through Assembly System

Herman Hertzberger has described the construction as made up of an assembly system, which is why the building can be altered without great effort: "Designing an office building may be simple in principle, but it was precisely the need for flexibility that mattered in this job. Continuous organizational changes require frequent adaptation to the size of the different divisions. The structure has to accommodate all these internal forces and still function in every respect and at all times as a whole. . . . Designed as an organized spatial complex, the building consists of a basic structure that essentially represents a fixed, permanent core and a variable expansion zone subject to reinterpretation."[10] For that reason the building's supporting skeleton was erected on a grid of supports with prefabricated concrete elements. The dominant materials outside and inside are light-colored concrete blocks. Together with the concrete, steel, and glass, the exposed masonry gives the spaces a friendly, stimulating feeling.

10 Herman Hertzberger: Vom Bauen. Vorlesungen über Architektur, München/Munich 1995, S./p. 129. Fortan zitiert als/cited below as Vom Bauen.

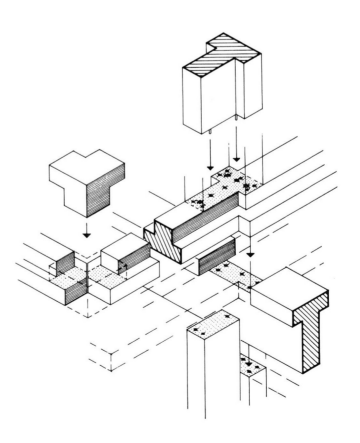

Die beiden Fotos zeigen die doppelstöckige, nach außen hin offene Tiefgarage unter dem Bürogebäude. Selbst solchen Bereichen verleiht Hertzberger eine ‚einladende Form' und sorgfältige Details.

These two photographs show the two-story parking garage beneath the office building and open to the outside. Hertzberger provided even such areas with an "inviting form" and exacting details.

Bekenntnis zu einfachen Materialien

Mit wenigen Ausnahmen hat Herman Hertzberger bei seinen Bauten in den 1970er und 1980er Jahren – als auch die Fotografien zu diesem Buch entstanden sind – die stets gleichen Materialien eingesetzt. Im Unterschied zu der gerade bei Bürogebäuden oder Kulturzentren üblichen Opulenz vertraut er auf den Gestaltwert einfacher Baustoffe wie Sichtbeton, Betonstein und Glasbaustein. Diese gleichwertigen, unaufdringlichen Materialien, im Detail ebenso sorgfältig wie variationsreich verarbeitet, geben seinen Bauten einen spröden Charme. Die Materialwahl wertet Hertzberger als ein entscheidendes Kriterium für architektonische Identität und Glaubwürdigkeit. In einem Gespräch mit den befreundeten Architekten des ‚Atelier 5' in der Schweiz sagte er: „Ich sehe die Gefahr, dass durch die allzu unbefangene Verwendung verschiedenster Materialien die Handschrift nicht mehr lesbar bleibt. Architektonische Handschrift hat etwas mit Beschränkung auf wenige Materialien zu tun. Es geht dabei vor allem um Zurückhaltung. (...) Ich persönlich habe immer ganz bewusst der Versuchung der ‚schönen' Materialien widerstanden."[11] Im weiteren Verlauf des Gesprächs räumt er ein: „Natürlich darf man sich von Zeit zu Zeit gewisse Extravaganzen erlauben, aber es muss untergeordnet bleiben, und ich muss es kontrollieren können. Entscheidend ist für mich, und das gilt auch für die Form, dass ich nur dann etwas Extravagantes tue, wenn dadurch auch bessere Ergebnisse möglich werden. Nie darf so etwas aus einer Laune oder aus Willkür geschehen."

Commitment to Simple Materials

With few exceptions, Herman Hertzberger consistently used the same materials in his buildings in the 1970s and 1980s—when the photographs for this book were taken. In contrast to the opulence typical of office buildings or cultural centers in particular, he relied on the design value of such simple building materials as exposed concrete, concrete blocks, and glass bricks. These compatible, unimposing materials, used meticulously and with great variation, give his buildings a demure charm. Hertzberger values his choice of materials as a decisive factor for his architectural identity and credibility. In a conversation in Switzerland with his architect friends at "Atelier 5" he said: "I see the danger that with an all-too-unrestrained use of the most varied materials one's signature is no longer legible. An architectural signature has something to do with a reduction to few materials. It has to do above all with restraint. . . . I myself have always quite deliberately resisted the temptation of "beautiful" materials."[11] In the further course of that conversation he confessed: "Naturally one can permit oneself certain extravagances from time to time, but this has to be subordinate, and I have to be able to control it. Decisive for me, and that is true for the form as well, is that I only do something extravagant if that allows for better results. That sort of thing must never be done on a whim or capriciously."

11 Herman Hertzberger in: Atelier 5, 26 ausgewählte Bauten, Zürich 1986, S./p. 10.

Ende eines Denkmals

Als die Zeitschrift ‚Bauwelt' im Jahr 2015 an das inzwischen leer stehende, aber sehr gut erhaltene Centraal Beheer als Sanierungsfall erinnerte, bestand noch die Hoffnung, das einzigartige Gebäude könne durch eine neue Nutzung gerettet werden.[12] Die Autorin Marika Schmidt schrieb damals: „Das Raumkonzept ist heute wahrscheinlich näher am Zeitgeist, als es je war. Beim Besuch denke ich unweigerlich an moderne Bibliotheken und Schulen – warum nur zieht hier die Medienbranche nicht ein?" Im Juli 2016 legte Herman Hertzberger ein eigenes Papier zur Zukunft des Gebäudes vor, unter anderem mit einem Vorschlag für studentisches Wohnen.[13] Doch alle Hoffnung war vergebens – 2018 beschloss der Gemeinderat, das Gebäude abzureißen und auf dem Gelände 350 Mietwohnungen zu errichten. Umso wichtiger sind heute die Aufnahmen von Klaus Kinold, der dieses Meisterwerk seinerzeit mit den Augen des ausgebildeten Architekten fotografisch dokumentierte und für die Nachwelt bewahrt hat. Herman Hertzberger schätzte Kinolds Empathie so sehr, dass er ihn als Fotograf für seine 1990 im Uitgeverij 010 Verlag erschienene Monografie auswählte.

12 Centraal Beheer in: Bauwelt, 2015, Heft/*issue* 5, S./*pp.* 22-29.
13 Herman Hertzberger: The Future of the Building ‚Centraal Beheer' [2016].

End of a Monument

When in 2015 the journal 'Bauwelt' evoked the Centraal Beheer—meanwhile deserted but very well preserved—as a case for restoration, there was still the hope that the unique structure could be saved through a new use.[12] The writer Marika Schmidt noted at that time: "Its concept of space is today probably closer to the spirit of the time than it ever was. On visiting it I automatically thought of modern libraries and schools—why couldn't a media company move in here?" In July 2016 Herman Hertzberger submitted a paper of his own on the future of the building, suggesting among other things the possibility of student housing.[13] But all hope was in vain—in 2018 the local council decided to raze the building and build 350 rental apartments on the site. All the more important today are the photographs by Klaus Kinold, who documented this masterpiece at the time with the eyes of a trained architect and preserved it for posterity. Herman Hertzberger valued Kinold's empathy so highly that he selected him as the photographer for his monograph published in 1990 by Uitgeverij 010 publishing house.

Die Aufnahmen zeigen den Blick auf eine Ecksituation sowie den Ausblick von einer Cafeteria in die angrenzende ‚Büroinsel'. Auf beiden Fotos ist die hohe Qualität der Detaillierung zu erkennen: bei der Außenwand die sichtbar belassene Konstruktion der Elemente, im Innenraum die liebevolle gestalterische Durcharbeitung bis hin zu den kleinen Tischen mit integrierten Leuchten.

These photographs show views of a corner situation from a cafeteria into the adjacent "office island." In both photographs one sees the high quality of the detailing: on the exterior wall the construction elements are left visible, in the interior everything is designed with care, down to the small tables with their attached lamps.

Die Baukunst besteht weder darin, nur schöne Dinge hervorzubringen, noch einzig nützliche – sie muß beides zugleich tun, wie der Schneider, der Kleider herstellt, die gut aussehen und auch passen. Und, wenn möglich, Kleider, die jeder tragen kann, nicht nur der Kaiser.

    Herman Hertzberger

The art of architecture is not only to make beautiful things – nor is it only to make useful things, it is to do both at once – like a tailor who makes clothes that both look good and fit well. And, if at all possible, clothes that everyone can wear, not just the Emperor.

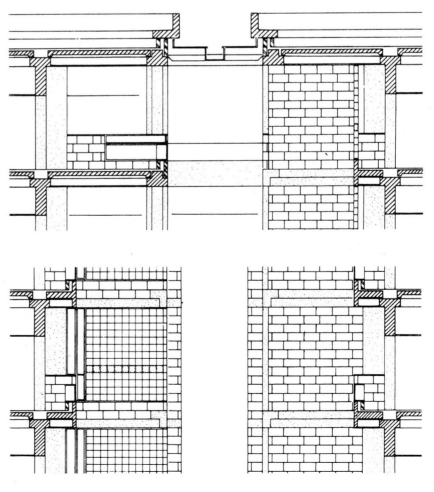

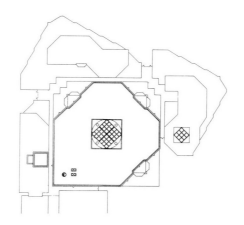 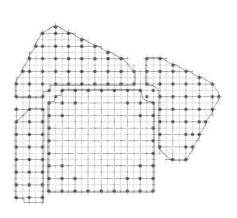

Musikzentrum Vredenburg
Utrecht, 1973–1978

Das Gebäude des Musikzentrums nimmt in der Innenstadt von Utrecht eine exponierte Lage ein. Es bildet den Übergang von einem Einkaufszentrum mit großer Geschäftspassage zur kleinteiligen Altstadt. Entsprechend wurde die Baumasse in mehrere Körper gegliedert. Der niedrigste Teil mit einem auskragenden Geschoss und Dachterrassen befindet sich am östlich gelegenen Platz ‚Vredenburg' gegenüber der Altstadt. Im Süden grenzt der Komplex an das Einkaufszentrum, an den beiden anderen Seiten ist er von breiten, viel befahrenen Straßen umgeben.

Anstelle eines isolierten ‚Musiktempels' entwarf Herman Hertzberger ein Gebäude, das räumlich und funktional eng mit der städtischen Struktur verwoben ist. Wie der linke Strukturplan zeigt, sind dem Großen Saal mit 1.700 Sitzplätzen als Zentrum der Anlage an drei Seiten flachere Zonen mit unterschiedlicher Nutzung vorgelagert. Diese überwiegend unregelmäßig geschnittenen Baukörper enthalten Läden, Restaurants, Büros und das städtische Informationszentrum. Zwischen ihnen und dem mächtigen Saalbau verlaufen ebenso lange wie schmale, aber hohe Passagen, die durch Glasbänder von oben belichtet werden. Arkaden, Galerien und Fußgängerbrücken gliedern die Passagen und schaffen erlebnisreiche Räume mit wechselnden Sichtbeziehungen. Den Großen Saal erreicht man nicht durch einen imposanten Haupteingang (auch darin besteht eine Parallele zu Centraal Beheer), sondern von mehreren Seiten ohne Hemmschwellen beim Gang durch die Passagen zu den weiträumigen, den Saal umfassenden Foyers im Erdgeschoss und im 1. Obergeschoss [Schnitt auf Seite 37]. Der achteckige, stufenförmig ansteigende Raum mit fast zentriertem Podium wird durch eine große Lichtkuppel erhellt, die von außen bei Tag und Nacht einen Blickpunkt darstellt [siehe Foto]. Eine Lichtkuppel hat auch der zweigeschossige Kleine Saal mit 250 Sitzplätzen.

Komplexer Funktionalismus
Das Musikzentrum ist nach Wessel Reinink „das lebhafteste seiner Art in den Niederlanden", weil es für eine breite Skala von Veranstaltungen genutzt werden kann.[14] In seiner Gestalt strebt es nach einer Balance zwischen Großform und Vielgliedrigkeit. Das Gebäude vereint

Music Center Vredenburg
Utrecht, 1973–1978

The Music Center building occupies a prominent site in inner-city Utrecht. It forms the transition from a shopping center with a large arcade to the small-scale Old Town. Accordingly, the main structure was divided into several components. The lowest section with a cantilevered floor and roof terraces stands on Vredenburg Square facing the Old Town on the east. On the south the complex borders the shopping center, on the other two sides it is flanked by heavily trafficked streets.

Instead of an isolated "temple of music," Herman Hertzberger designed a building that is closely tied, both spatially and functionally, to the urban substance. As shown in the plan on the left, flatter sections with varied functions are nestled against the large, 1,700-seat hall at the center of the complex. These largely irregular-shaped sections house shops, restaurants, offices, and the municipal information center. Between them and the massive hall run long, narrow passageways illuminated from high above by ribbons of glass. Arcades, galleries, and pedestrian bridges break up the passageways and create exciting spaces with changing views. One reaches the large hall not through an imposing main entrance (another parallel to Centraal Beheer), but through spacious foyers on the ground and second floors off the surrounding passageways (cross section on p. 37). The octagonal, stepped hall with its almost centered podium is illuminated by a square glass dome, which serves as a focal point day and night (see photograph). The two-story smaller hall with seating for 250 also has a glass dome.

Complex Functionalism
According to Wessel Reinink, the Music Center is "the liveliest of its kind in the Netherlands," as it can be used for a broad range of events.[14] In its structure it attempts to strike a balance between monumental form and fragmentation. It combines three of Hertzberger's fundamental principles. First: a public building, especially, has to seem "anti-monumental" and fit in with the city dwellers' everyday lives. Second: as opposed to the rigid division of functions in urban planning promoted by CIAM ever since its "Athens Charter" in 1933, Hertzberger argues for an imaginative overlapping of functions—a building has to be perceived as a "miniature

drei Grundprinzipien von Hertzberger. Erstens: Vor allem ein öffentliches Bauwerk müsse ‚anti-monumental' auftreten und sich in den lebendigen Alltag der Stadtbewohner einfügen. Zweitens: Entgegen der rigiden Funktionstrennung im Städtebau, wie sie von der CIAM seit ihrer ‚Charta von Athen' aus dem Jahr 1933 gepredigt wurde, plädiert Hertzberger für die phantasievolle Überlagerung von Funktionen – ein Gebäude müsse wie eine ‚kleine Stadt' verstanden werden. Aus diesem ‚komplexen' Funktionalismus folgt drittens sein Streben nach der ‚polyvalenten Form' mit dem Angebot, dass das Bauwerk individuell gedeutet und angeeignet werden kann. Im Unterschied zu Centraal Beheer wurde das Musikzentrum in den Niederlanden kontrovers aufgefasst – man kritisierte sowohl die zerklüftete Großform ohne eigentliche Fassaden als auch das ‚labyrinthische' Raumgefüge. Selbstkritisch räumte Hertzberger ein, dass „mehr auf die Lesbarkeit der Teile als auf den Zusammenhang des Ganzen geachtet" wurde.[15]

city." From this "complex" functionalism, thirdly, follows his striving for "polyvalent form," with the proposition that a structure can be individually interpreted and appropriated. In contrast to Centraal Beheer, the Music Center aroused controversy in the Netherlands—it was criticized both for its fragmented overall form, lacking real facades, and for its "labyrinthine" arrangement of spaces. Hertzberger concedes that he paid "more attention to the legibility of its parts than to the coherence of the whole."[15]

14 Reinink: Hertzberger, S./p. III.
15 Vom Bauen, S./p. 132.

30

Das strukturelle Grundprinzip vermitteln die konstruktiven Kreuzungspunkte. Jede der Möglichkeiten ist eine Abwandlung des gleichen Prinzips, wie die Konjugation eines Verbs von seiner Grundform. Zusammen bilden die verschiedenen Varianten eine Art Grammatik: Baukonstruktion als architektonisches Ordnungsprinzip.

Constructive intersections provide the fundamental structural principle. Each of the possibilities is a variation on the same principle, like a verb's conjugations from its stem. Together the different variants form a kind of grammar: building construction as a principle of architectural arrangement.

Herman Hertzberger

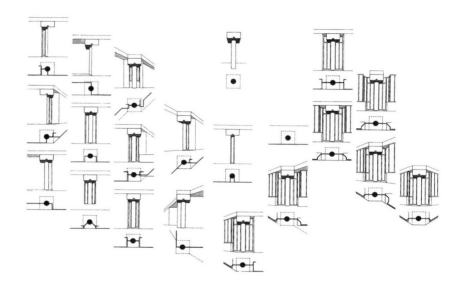

Bei Gratis-Konzerten sind im Erdgeschoss die breiten Schwenktüren zum Großen Saal ganz geöffnet, um auch Passanten zum Besuch der Aufführungen anzuregen – Foyer und Saal gehen dann ineinander über.

At free concerts the wide swinging doors on the ground floor are opened completely to encourage passersby to attend the performance—foyer and hall flow into each other.

Hülle und Kern

Mit dem Großen Saal des Musikzentrums hatte Hertzberger erstmals einen derart großen Raum zu entwerfen. Der nebenstehende Schnitt verdeutlicht, wie der in Stufen ansteigende Saal als Kern des Gebäudes von den vielfältigen Funktionen in den flacheren Bauteilen umhüllt ist. Rechts von ihm liegt der Kleine Saal mit ebenfalls einer Lichtkuppel. Alle Baukörper wurden auf einem konsequenten Stützenraster errichtet. Ein markantes Element sind die unverkleideten Betonsäulen mit kubischen Stützenköpfen. Herman Hertzberger hat sie erläutert: „Bei frei stehenden Säulen sind die runden zweifellos vorzuziehen, sei es nur, weil sie sich in überfüllte Räume freundlicher und sanfter einfügen. Überall ‚im Weg' stehend, behaupten sie sich mit voller Kraft, während die viereckigen Kapitelle, eine ‚Überbetonung' der konstruktionsbedingten Form, ihre Präsenz noch hervorheben."[16]

Case and Core

The Great Hall of the Music Center was Hertzberger's first design for such a large space. The cross section on the right shows how the hall, rising in steps, is ringed by multiple functions in the flatter building sections. To the right of it is the Small Hall with its own glass dome. All of the structure's components were erected on a standard grid of supports. Striking features are the exposed concrete columns with their cubical capitals. Herman Hertzberger explained them: "For free-standing columns round ones are unquestionably preferable, if only because they seem friendlier in crowded spaces and fit in more easily. Standing everywhere 'in the way,' they assert themselves with full strength, while the square capitals, an "overemphasis" on construction-dictated form, only further accentuate them."[16]

16 Vom Bauen, S./p. 133.

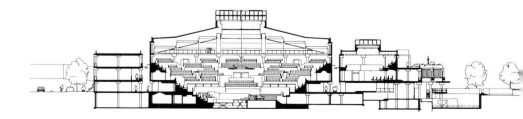

Apollo-Schulen
Amsterdam, 1980–1983

Den berühmt gewordenen Schulbauten von Herman Hertzberger sieht man auf den ersten Blick ihren Kontext mit den Zielen der Reformpädagogik an. Das äußert sich in der räumlichen Gliederung, in der sich daraus ergebenden differenzierten Gestalt der Baukörper sowie in den zahlreichen kinderfreundlichen Details.

Bei den als Paar geplanten Apollo-Schulen[17] ist außerdem eine harmonische Einfügung in das städtische Umfeld geglückt: Die dreigeschossigen villenartigen Gebäude nehmen typologisch den Charakter des durchgrünten Wohngebiets auf. Wie die Isometrie zeigt, öffnen sich die rechtwinklig zueinander liegenden Schulen mit integrierten Kindergärten sowohl zum gemeinsamen Schulhof als auch zum rückwärtigen Spielplatz: links die Montessori-Schule, rechts die Willemspark-Schule. Die beiden Bauten sind weitgehend identisch. Unterschiede ergaben sich aufgrund der anderen Lage auf dem Grundstück bei der Anordnung der Fenster und der Ausbildung der Gebäudeecken. Strukturell haben sie den gleichen Aufbau [Schnitte nächste Seite]. Zentrum jeder Schule ist eine mehrgeschossige, von oben belichtete Halle. Auf zwei Seiten steigen die Klassenräume, jeweils paarweise versetzt, bis zum Dachgeschoss an, wo Terrassen den Unterricht im Freien ermöglichen. Das Foto zeigt die Gebäudeecke am Zugang zur Montessori-Schule mit dem prägenden Sichtmauerwerk aus hellen Betonsteinen, dessen feinporige Struktur durch das wandernde Tageslicht akzentuiert wird.

The Apollo Schools
Amsterdam, 1980–1983

In Herman Hertzberger's now famous school buildings one sees at first glance their commitment to educational reform. This is expressed in their spatial arrangement, in the resulting differentiated shapes of the building elements, and in the countless child-friendly details.

A harmonious incorporation into the urban surroundings was also accomplished in the Apollo Schools.[17] Planned as a pair, the three-story, villa-like structures take on the character of the greenery-filled residential quarter. As the isometric drawing shows, the two schools with their integrated kindergartens stand at right angles to each other, opening onto a common courtyard as well as to a playground at the back. On the left is the Montessori School, on the right the Willemspark School. The two buildings are largely identical. Differences in the window arrangement and the formation of the building corners were the result of their positions on the site. Structurally, they are identical (cross section page 42). The core of each school is a multi-story hall lit from above. On two sides the classrooms, set back in pairs, extend up to the top floor, where terraces make teaching outdoors a possibility. The photograph shows the building's corner at the entrance to the Montessori School with its prominently exposed masonry of light-colored concrete blocks, their porous texture accentuated by the changing play of light.

17 Heinz Jakubeit: Apollo-Schulen in Amsterdam, in Klaus Kinold (Hg./ed.): Bauen in Beton/Construire en béton, Heft/issue 1/86, München/Munich 1986, S./pp. 10-17.

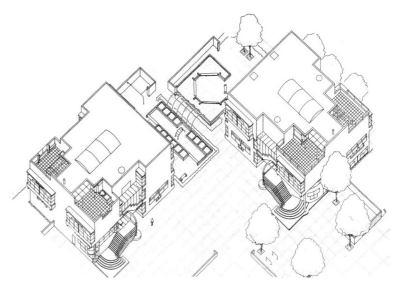

Beide Schulbauten wirken wie große Wohnhäuser. Bandartige Fenster öffnen sich zu den Straßen wie zum geschützten Hof, kleine Balkone und vorkragende Geschosse greifen über die Baukörper hinaus, großzügige Außentreppen leiten zu den erhöhten, durch Vordächer geschützten Eingängen – mit ihrer Erscheinung laden die Schulen zum Besuch ein.

The school buildings resemble large blocks of apartments. Ribbon windows open onto the streets and the protected courtyard, small balconies and cantilevered floors break up the bulk of the structures, and broad flights of stairs lead up to entrances protected by projecting roofs. The schools' appearance invites visitors to enter.

Gebäudeschnitte: links die Montessori- und rechts die Willemspark-Schule.

Cross sections: the Montessori School on the left, the Willemspark School on the right.

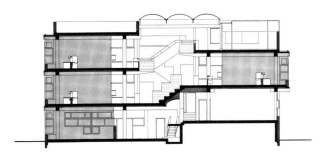

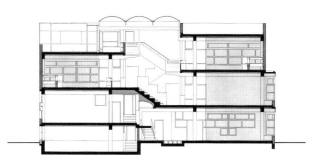

In seinem Buch ‚Vom Bauen' hat sich Hertzberger auch zur Detaillierung seiner Brüstungen geäußert: „Wir machen keine Brüstungen mit fließenden Linien, die aus ellenlangen, zusammengeschweißten Metallröhren oder Profilstangen bestehen, sondern versuchen, sie aus einzelnen Komponenten zu formen." [Seite 238] Rechts im Foto der Balkon an der Willemspark-Schule.

In his book 'Vom Bauen' Hertzberger also explained the detailing of his railings: "We do not make railings with flowing lines consisting of welded metal pipes or profiled bars, but rather try to form them out of individual components." [page 238] On the right in the photograph is the balcony of the Willemspark School.

Grundrisse der Willemspark-Schule: Eingangsgeschoss, 1. und 2. Obergeschoss.

Ground plans of the Willemspark School: Ground, second, and third floors.

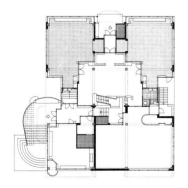
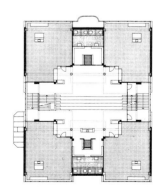
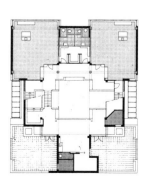

Benutzer werden Bewohner

Insbesondere beim Entwurf seiner Schulbauten suchte Herman Hertzberger die Mitwirkung der künftigen Benutzer. Partizipation verpflichtet aber nicht nur den Architekten, sondern auch die jeweilige ‚Schulfamilie', von der ein achtsamer Umgang mit dem Gebäude erwartet wird: „Schon bei der Planung der Grundrisse und Schnitte sowie durch das Konstruktionsprinzip können Bedingungen geschaffen werden, die das Verantwortungsgefühl steigern und ein größeres Engagement bei der Anordnung und Möblierung bestimmter Bereiche hervorrufen. Der Benutzer wird zum Bewohner."[18] Für das Angebot an die Schüler, sich mit ihren Räumen zu identifizieren, weil sie diese mitgestalten können, dann aber auch entsprechend pflegen sollen, verwendet Hertzberger die Metapher vom ‚Nest' [Zitat Seite 52]. Diese Metapher lag bereits den Arbeitsplätzen im Centraal Beheer zugrunde – welch ein Kontrast zur Situation heutiger Angestellter, die sich wie Nomaden in den Bürohäusern zu bewegen haben.

18 Vom Bauen, S./p. 26.

Users become Inhabitants

In the design especially of his school buildings Herman Hertzberger invites collaboration from their future occupants. Participation obliges not only the architect, however, but also the given "school family," from whom careful treatment of the building is expected. "Even in the design of the ground plans and cross sections, as well as in the principle of construction, situations can be created that enhance the feeling of responsibility, and call forth greater engagement with the arrangement and furnishing of specific areas. The user becomes an inhabitant."[18] When offering pupils a chance to identify with their spaces and ultimately take care of them by helping to design them, Hertzberger made use of the "nest" metaphor [quote page 52]. It was already behind the work spaces in the Centraal Beheer—a distinct contrast to the plight of today's employees forced to range about in office buildings like nomads.

Die Grundrisse der Montessori-
Schule: Eingangsgeschoss,
1. und 2. Obergeschoss.

Ground plans of the Montessori
School: Ground, second, and
third floors.

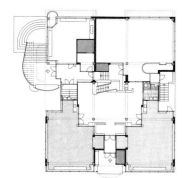
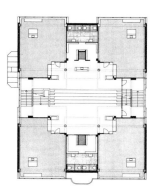
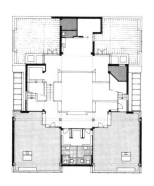

Die Halle funktioniert wie ein großes gemeinsames Klassenzimmer...

Herman Hertzberger

The hall space functions rather like a big communal classroom...

Ein ‚sicheres Nest' – eine vertraute Umgebung, von der man weiß, dass dort die eigenen Sachen sicher aufgehoben sind, und in der man sich konzentrieren kann, ohne durch andere gestört zu werden – ist etwas, was jeder Mensch braucht, sei es der Einzelne oder die Gruppe. Ohne dies ist kein Zusammenarbeiten mit den anderen möglich. Wer keinen Platz hat, den er als seinen eigenen betrachten kann, weiß nicht, wo er steht!

A "safe nest" – familiar surroundings where you know that your things are safe and where you can concentrate without being disturbed by others – is something that each individual needs as much as a group. Without this there can be no collaboration with others. If you don't have a place that you can call your own you don't know where you stand.

Herman Hertzberger

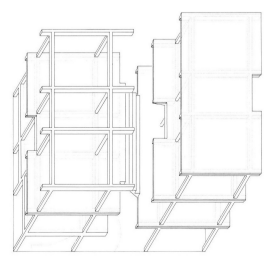

53

Differenziert gestaltete Treppen und Ecksituationen spielen bei den Apollo-Schulen eine große Rolle. Sie bieten Sitzgelegenheiten an und laden rund um Stützen oder Säulen zum ungezwungenen Spiel ein.

Carefully designed stairs and corner areas are important features of the Apollo Schools. They offer seating opportunities and invite spontaneous play around supports or columns.

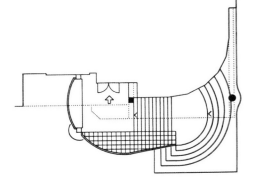

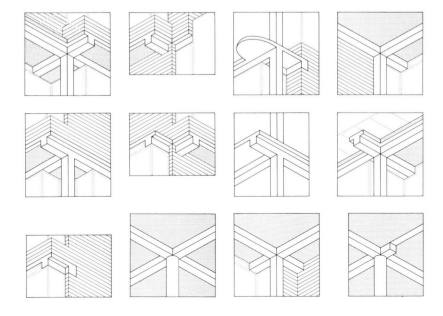

Auswahl von möglichen Anschlüssen und Verbindungen im Konstruktionssystem der beiden Schulen.

A selection of possible abutments and ties in the construction system of the two schools.

Raumökonomie mit Transparenz

Die beiden Fotos zeigen neben der konsequenten und zugleich unaufdringlichen Gestaltung durch wenige Materialien eine geschickte Raumökonomie ohne ‚tote Ecken'. Verglaste Wandfelder sorgen immer wieder für großzügige Durchblicke in benachbarte Räume und Bereiche. Herman Hertzberger spricht von der ‚gemeinsamen Grammatik' beider Schulen: „Das zugrunde liegende Konstruktionsprinzip umfasst etwa 20 Punkte, die sich je nach ihrer Interpretationsmöglichkeit wie folgt einordnen lassen: innen-außen, Skelett oder konsequente Anwendung von Mauersteinen, Simsen oder Stahlelementen, Normalgröße oder Überdimensionierung, Quer- oder T-Träger. Alle Teile sind durch eine Art Verwandtschaft verbunden."[19]

Economy of Space with Transparency

In addition to logical and unobtrusive design with limited materials, these two photographs illustrate a deft economy of space without "dead corners." Glass wall panels again and again provide generous views into neighboring spaces and sectors. Herman Hertzberger speaks of the "common grammar" of the two schools: "The construction principle on which they are based incorporates some 20 points, which can be arranged, depending on their possible interpretation, as follows: interior–exterior, skeleton, or consistent use of concrete blocks, cornices or steel elements, normal or oversized, cross or T girders. All the parts are tied together by a kind of affinity."[19]

19 Vom Bauen, S./p. 139.

Schule De Evenaar
Amsterdam, 1984–1986

Als Weiterentwicklung des bei den Apollo-Schulen ausgeführten Grundrissprinzips, welches das gemeinsame Lernen fördern soll, kann die Primarschule De Evenaar im Osten von Amsterdam gelten.[20] Dieses Gebäude, inmitten eines dicht bebauten Wohnviertels gelegen, enthält neun Klassenzimmer, die in Dreiergruppen um einen Kern mit zentraler Halle und Aufenthaltsräumen gelegt sind.

Das trotz seiner auffälligen Dreigliedrigkeit geschlossen wirkende Schulhaus liegt auf dem Ambonplein, einem kleinen Platz, der den Mittelpunkt des Viertels bildet. Wie eine Plastik steht es nach allen Seiten hin frei. Die überwiegend verglasten Fassaden der Klassenräume orientieren sich nach Osten und Westen. Im Kontrast zu den horizontal betonten Flügeln stellt der durch das völlig verglaste Treppenhaus geprägte Mittelteil einen vertikalen Akzent dar. Um dieses ‚Herzstück' steigen die Klassenräume spiralförmig bis zum Dachgeschoss an. Vor dem Haupteingang mit der Außentreppe befindet sich ein großer, auch Kindern und Jugendlichen aus der Nachbarschaft zugänglicher Schulhof, im Süden vor dem Eingang des Kindergartens ein Spielplatz. Die frei gestaltete Außentreppe ist in der Achse zweifach versetzt. Entscheidend für Gestalt und Organisation des Gebäudes ist die Dialektik von Zentrum und Peripherie. Alle möglichen Aktivitäten laufen in der zentralen Halle zusammen, während die Klassenräume in den erkerförmig vorspringenden Seitenflügeln ein ungestörtes Lehren und Lernen ermöglichen. Diese Bereiche sind aber nicht abgeschlossen, sondern mit dem Zentrum durch Sitzplätze, Treppenanlagen und teilverglaste Innenwände verbunden. Durch die Verschränkung der verschiedenen Ebenen, die erlebnisreichen Durchblicke bis in die städtische Umgebung hinein und die großteils transparente Hülle des Baukörpers ergibt sich ein sozial anregendes Ambiente.

[20] Wolfgang Jean Stock: Schule ‚De Evenaar' in Amsterdam-Ost, in Klaus Kinold (Hg./ed.): MODUL – Betonsteine in der neuen Architektur, Heft/issue 3, München/Munich 1988, S./pp. 13-23. Ders./Idem: Schule ‚De Evenaar' in Amsterdam, in Klaus Kinold (Hg./ed.): Architektur und Beton, Ostfildern 1994, S./pp. 88-95.

De Evenaar School
Amsterdam, 1984–1986

The De Evenaar primary school on the east side of Amsterdam can be seen as a further development of the fundamental principle followed in the Apollo Schools, one intended to foster communal learning.[20] This building, situated in the midst of a densely built-up residential quarter, holds nine classrooms ranged in groups of three around a core with a central hall and recreation rooms.

The school building, which seems compact despite its obvious three-part structure, stands on the Ambonplein, a small square that forms the quarter's center. Like a sculpture, it is exposed on all sides. The facades of the classrooms, mostly glass, are oriented to the east and west. In contrast to the dominant horizontals of the wings, the center section with its wholly glazed stairwell serves as a vertical accent. Around this core the classrooms rise in a spiral up to the top floor. In front of the main entrance with its open staircase a large courtyard is equally accessible to children and young people from the neighborhood, and in front of the south entrance there is a playground. The exterior stairs are twice offset from their axis. Decisive for the design and organization of the building is the dialectic between core and periphery. All sorts of activities take place in the central hall, whereas the classrooms in the oriel-shaped, projecting side wings allow for undisturbed teaching and learning. These areas are not closed off, however, but rather connected with the center by way of seating places, staircases, and partially glazed interior walls. Thanks to the ties between the various levels, the fascinating views out into the urban surroundings, and the structure's largely transparent shell, a stimulating social atmosphere is created.

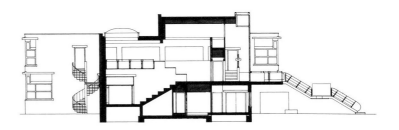

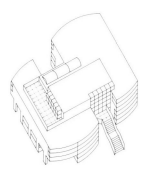

Das ebenso transparente wie kompakte, an ein ‚Schiff' erinnernde Schulhaus hebt sich durch eine andere Material- und Farbwahl, wofür auch die hellen Betonsteine stehen, von der umgebenden Wohnbebauung deutlich ab.

The school building, both transparent, compact, and reminiscent of a ship, clearly stands out from the surrounding residential substance with its different materials and coloring, namely the light gray concrete blocks.

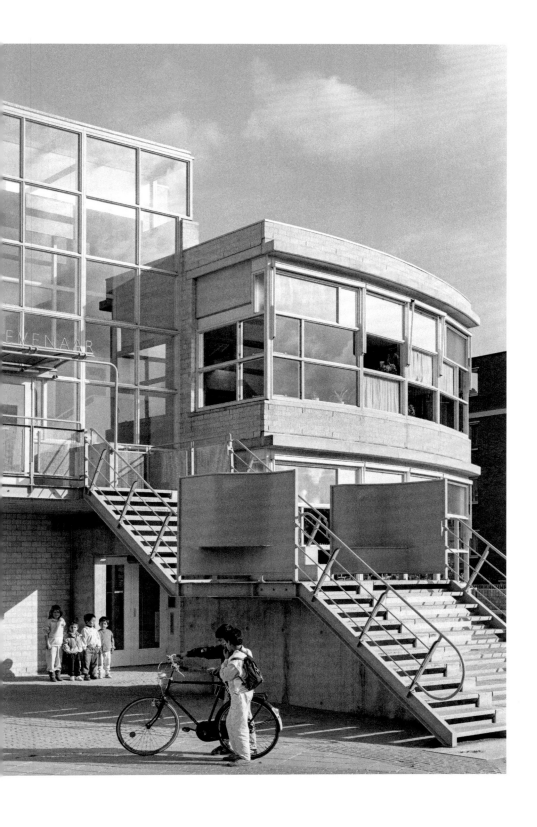

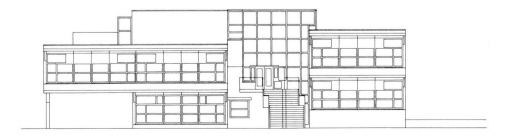

Aus den Klassenzimmern wie aus dem Spielraum im Erdgeschoss kann man ungehindert ins Freie schauen. Die fast geschosshohen Fensterbänder sorgen auch für eine großzügige Belichtung der Räume. Die breiten Fensterbänke und die zu Regalen erweiterten Profile dienen zum Aufstellen von Pflanzen, persönlichen Geräten oder Bastelarbeiten.

It is possible to look outside from each of the classrooms and well as from the playroom on the ground floor. The almost floor-to-ceiling rows of windows provide generous illumination. Broad window seats and moldings wide as shelves hold plants, personal objects, and craft projects.

Die Grundrisse der Schule De Evenaar: Erdgeschoss, Obergeschoss und Dachgeschoss.

De Evenaar ground plans: ground, second, and third floors.

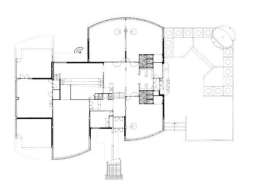
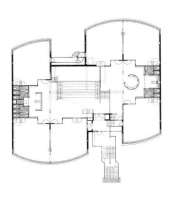
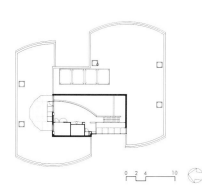

Wie bei den früheren Schulbauten von Hertzberger bildet auch hier die von allen Seiten zugängliche Halle das Zentrum. Die kleine Tribüne mit breiten Sitzstufen dient für Konzerte und andere Veranstaltungen.

As in Hertzberger's previous school buildings, a hall accessible from all sides forms the core. The small tribune with wide stairs to sit on serves for concerts and other performances.

Inszenierte Zugänge

Auch bei De Evenaar hat Herman Hertzberger die Außentreppe aus gutem Grund inszeniert: „Die zum Eingang der neuen Volksschule führende Treppe wurde besonders gegliedert, um den Zugang von der Straßenebene aus zu erleichtern. Da sich beide Treppenläufe nebeneinander befinden, lag es nah, die Geländerteile miteinander zu verbinden, was zum Entschluss führte, die Brüstungselemente im abgerundeten Treppenabsatz so auszubilden, dass zwei kleine Sitzplätze entstehen."[21] Das rechte Foto zeigt die sorgfältige Detaillierung der Glaswand des Treppenhauses mit eigens entworfener Leuchte.

Staged Entrances

For De Evenaar Herman Hertzberger likewise took care with the design of the exterior stairs for good reason: "The stairs leading to the entrance of the new grammar school were specially designed to facilitate access from the street level. Since the two flights of stairs are side by side, it made sense to combine the railing elements, which led to the decision to design them in such a way that two small seats are created on the rounded landings."[21] The photo on the right shows the careful detailing of the glass wall in the stairwell with a custom-designed lamp.

21 Vom Bauen, S./p. 178.

67

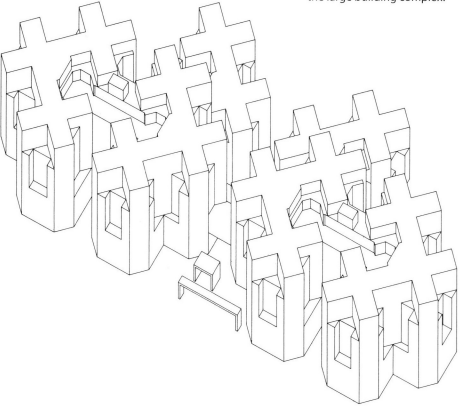

Die schematische Darstellung zeigt die charakteristische Gliederung des großen Gebäudekomplexes.

The schematic drawing shows the unusual arrangement of the large building complex.

Sozial- und Arbeitsministerium
Den Haag, 1979–1990

Das Ministeriumsgebäude für 2.000 Beschäftigte, dessen lange Bearbeitungszeit durch zunächst unterschiedliche Vorstellungen von Planer und Nutzern verursacht wurde, blieb Hertzbergers größtes Projekt. Er selbst hat es selbstironisch als „freundliche Burg" bezeichnet. Der Autor Wessel Reinink sieht im Ministeriumsbau „das Ende einer Entwicklungsphase seines Schaffens".[22]

Ziel des Architekten war „ein offenes Gebäude für eine offene Behörde". Diese Konzeption ließ sich trotz der geforderten Kompromisse im Wesentlichen verwirklichen. Das trotz der vielen Einschnitte und ‚Auskantungen' kompakt wirkende Bauwerk liegt außerhalb des Stadtzentrums von Den Haag zwischen einem Bahnhof im Süden und einem niedrig bebauten Wohnviertel im Norden, von dem es durch einen kleinen Park entlang des Flüsschens Schenk Abstand hält. Der fast 200 Meter lange und 100 Meter breite Komplex gliedert sich in drei Abschnitte. Sechzehn achteckige Türme mit außen liegenden, verglasten Fluchttreppenhäusern sind kreuzweise miteinander verknüpft, wobei die quer durchlaufende Halle als halböffentliches ‚Rückgrat' die beiden Flügel mit dem zentralen Bereich verbindet. Gegenüber der Wohnbebauung fallen die ansonsten neungeschossigen Türme auf sechs Stockwerke ab. Aufgrund der Sicherheitsvorschriften hatte sich Hertzberger erstmals für einen mittigen Haupteingang entschieden, der gegenüber dem Bahnhof durch einen Torbau für Fußgänger und Autofahrer betont ist [siehe Foto]. Vom ebenerdigen Eingangsbereich gelangt man über Rolltreppen in den zentralen Hallenraum. Von dort führen wiederum Rolltreppen in die seitlichen Hallen der beiden Flügel, die ansonsten nur noch im obersten Bürogeschoss durch eine schmale Brücke über dem zentralen Bereich verbunden sind. Die Geschosse der Türme mit je dreißig Arbeitsplätzen lassen sich flexibel von Einzelbüros bis zu Großraumflächen unterteilen. Das elementierte Betonskelett auf einem Stützenraster mit diagonal laufenden Hauptträgern wurde bei den geschlossenen Wandfeldern mit einem Sichtmauerwerk aus hellgrauen Betonsteinen ausgefacht. Das Fugennetz der Steine gliedert die Fassaden und relativiert den großen Maßstab der Baukörper.

Ministry of Social Affairs and Employment
The Hague, 1979–1990

The construction of this building for a ministry with 2,000 employees was repeatedly delayed by disagreements between planners and users. It has remained Hertzberger's largest project. Self-deprecatingly, he himself refers to it as a "friendly fortress." The writer Wessel Reinink saw the ministry complex as "the end of one phase in the development of his work."[22]

The architect's goal was "an open structure for an open authority." And despite the changes required, that concept was essentially realized. The structure, which seems compact despite the many indentations and projecting angles, lies outside The Hague's city center, between a train station to the south and a low-rise residential section to the north, from which it is set apart by a small park along the little stream Schenk. Nearly 200 meters long and 100 meters wide, the complex is divided into three sections. Sixteen octagonal towers with exterior glass stairwells are tied together crosswise, a transverse hall tying the two wings to the central area as a half-open "spine." Facing the residential buildings the otherwise nine-story towers are reduced to six. Because of safety regulations Hertzberger for the first time opted for a central main entrance, one that is emphasized across from the train station by a gate-like structure for pedestrians and cars (see photo). From the ground-floor entry area one reaches the central hall space via escalator. From there additional escalators lead to the side halls of the two wings, otherwise connected only by a narrow bridge across the central space. The tower floors, each with three work spaces, can be flexibly divided, turned into single offices or large open spaces. The basic concrete skeleton on a grid of supports with diagonal girders was filled in with exposed masonry of light gray concrete blocks. Their network of joints patterns the facades and breaks up the structure's large scale.

Ein Menschenfreund

Der Autor hat Hertzberger erstmals 1985 erlebt, beim Architektentag in Frankfurt am Main. Von dessen Auftritt war er so begeistert wie die über eintausend Zuhörer: „Die Forderung, Architektur nach ihrem Gebrauchswert zu beurteilen, wurde vom holländischen Architekten Herman Hertzberger in einem frei gehaltenen, immer wieder von Beifall unterbrochenen Diavortrag glänzend belegt. Anhand von nur vier Beispielen aus seiner Arbeit entwickelte er die Grundsätze für ein menschengerechtes Bauen, die so einleuchtend sind wie sie in der Regel missachtet werden. Sein Bekenntnis zur ästhetischen Bescheidenheit im Geist der unverbrauchten Moderne enthielt eine witzig formulierte Kritik an krampfhafter Originalität: ‚Wenn die Postmodernisten erst Indien entdecken, sind wir ganz verloren. Glücklicherweise sind sie bisher nur bis Rom gekommen'."[23] Seither hat der Autor dem Menschenfreund zahlreiche Texte gewidmet, darunter einen Überblick über sein strukturalistisches Werk in der Schriftenreihe zur Verwendung von Betonsteinen.[24]

A Humanist

I first met Hertzberger in 1985, at the architects' conference in Frankfurt am Main. I was as enthusiastic about his lecture as was the audience of more than a thousand: "The demand that architecture be judged according to its usefulness was brilliantly argued by the Dutch architect Herman Hertzberger in an improvisatory slide show interrupted again and again by applause. Based on only four examples from his own work he developed the fundamental rules for human-scale building, rules as sensible as they are generally ignored. His commitment to aesthetic reticence in the spirit of still relevant Modernity included a wittily formulated criticism of forced originality: 'If the Postmodernists ever discover India we are utterly lost. Fortunately, as yet they have only got as far as Rome.'"[23] Since then I have devoted a number of texts to this user-focused architect, among them an overview of his structuralist work in the series on the use of concrete blocks.[24]

22 Wessel Reinink: Herman Hertzberger, in Klaus Kinold (Hg./ed.): Bauen in Beton/Construire en béton, Heft/issue 1995, München/Munich 1995, S./p. 7.
23 Wolfgang Jean Stock: Lebensraum Stadt. Der 6. Deutsche Architektentag in Frankfurt am Main, in: Süddeutsche Zeitung, Feuilleton, 8. Oktober 1985.
24 Wolfgang Jean Stock: Herman Hertzberger. Bauten 1968–1990, in Klaus Kinold (Hg./ed.): MODUL – Betonsteine in der neuen Architektur, Heft/issue 5, München/Munich 1992, S./pp. 2-19.

Auswahl von möglichen Anschlüssen und Verbindungen im Konstruktionssystem des Gebäudes.

Selection of possible abutments and ties in the building's structural system.

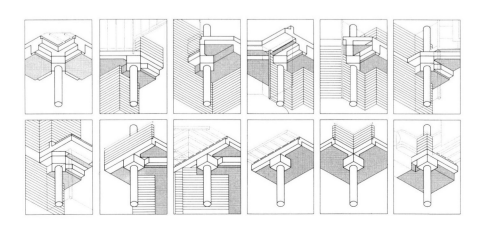

Dass die Architekten der Meinung sind, sie hätten sich nur mit dem Außergewöhnlichen zu befassen, ist ein weit verbreitetes Missverständnis: Sie bringen das Außergewöhnliche auf das Niveau des Gewöhnlichen, statt das Gewöhnliche außergewöhnlich zu gestalten.

Herman Hertzberger

It is a widespread misconception among architects that they should concern themselves with the extraordinary, i.e. that they bring the exceptional down to the level of the ordinary instead of rendering the ordinary extraordinary.

Die Aufnahmen zeigen die Verbindungen zwischen dem unverkleideten Betonskelett und dem strapazierfähigen Sichtmauerwerk aus hellgrauen Betonsteinen, das in den Innenräumen als ein angenehm neutraler Hintergrund wirkt. Sensibel gegliederte Tür- und Fensterelemente mit schmalen Profilen geben den Gängen und Fluren eine offene und heitere Note. Das untere Foto zeigt einen Blick in die quer durchlaufende Halle.

The photographs show the conjunctions between the exposed concrete skeleton and the sturdy bare masonry of light gray concrete blocks, which serves as a pleasantly neutral background in the interior spaces. Sensitively structured door and window elements with slender moldings give the corridors and vestibules an open and cheerful feeling. The photograph below shows one of the transverse halls.

Wir sind also nicht frei, willkürliche Formen zu entwerfen. Alles hat Konsequenzen für die Menschen und ihre Beziehungen. Wenn ein Architekt das Gefühl hat, mit seiner Arbeit die Welt doch nicht verbessern zu können, dann sollte er mindestens dafür sorgen, daß sie auch nicht schlechter wird.

Herman Hertzberger

We are therefore not free to go ahead and design whatever we like: everything has consequences for people and the relationships between them. If you do not believe that you can help to make the world a better place, you can at least make sure that you don't make it worse.

Herman Hertzberger

1932	geboren am 6. Juli in Amsterdam, Niederlande	Born July 6 in Amsterdam, the Netherlands
1958	Studium und Abschluss an der Technischen Universität Delft. Gründung des eigenen Büros in Amsterdam	Studies at and graduates from Delft University of Technology. Establishes his own office in Amsterdam
1959–1963	Redakteur der Zeitschrift FORUM, zusammen mit Aldo van Eyck, Jaap Bakema und anderen	Edits the journal FORUM together with Aldo van Eyck, Jaap Bakema, and others
1965–1969	Lehrer an der Architekturakademie in Amsterdam	Teaches at the Academy of Architecture, Amsterdam
1966–1996	Gastprofessor an verschiedenen Hochschulen in Kanada und den USA	Serves as visiting professor at several American and Canadian universities
1970–1999	Professor an der Technischen Universität in Delft	Appointed professor at Delft University of Technology
1975	Ehrenmitglied der Académie Royale de Belgique	Made an honorary member of the Académie Royale de Belgique
1982–1986	Gastprofessor an der Université de Genève, Schweiz	Serves as visiting professor at the University of Geneva, Switzerland
1983	Ehrenmitglied des Bundes Deutscher Architekten	Becomes an honorary member of the Bund Deutscher Architekten
1986–1993	Professor an der Université de Genève, Schweiz	Appointed a professor at the University of Geneva, Switzerland
1990–1995	Vorsitzender des Berlage Institute Amsterdam	Serves as chairman of the Berlage Institute, Amsterdam
1991	Officier in de Orde van Oranje Nassau (Ritter des Ordens von Oranien-Nassau)	Named a Knight of the Order of Orange-Nassau
1991	Ehrenmitglied des Royal Institute of British Architects (jetzt: International Fellow RIBA)	Named an honorary fellow of the Royal Institute of British Architects (now International Fellow RIBA)
1993	Ehrenmitglied der Akademie der Künste Berlin, Deutschland	Named an honorary member of the Akademie der Künste, Berlin
1995	Ehrenmitglied der Accademia delle Arti del Disegno Firenze, Italien	Named an honorary member of the Accademia delle Arti del Disegno, Florence
1996	Ehrenmitglied der Royal Incorporation of Architects in Scotland	Named an honorary fellow of the Royal Incorporation of Architects in Scotland
1997	Ehrenmitglied der Académie d'Architecture de France	Named an honorary member of the Académie d'Architecture de France
1999	Ridder in de Orde van de Nederlandse Leeuw (Ritter des Ordens vom Niederländischen Löwen)	Becomes a Ridder in de Orde van de Nederlandse Leeuw (Companion of the Order of the Dutch Lion)
1999–2000	Lehrer am Berlage Institute Amsterdam	Teaches at the Berlage Institute, Amsterdam
2001	Ehrendoktor (doctor honoris causa) der Université de Genève, Schweiz	Awarded an honorary doctorate by the University of Geneva, Switzerland
2002	Ehrenmitglied des Bond van Nederlandse Architecten (BNA)	Named an honorary member of the Bond van Nederlandse Architecten (BNA)
2004	Ehrenmitglied des American Institute of Architects (AIA)	Named an honorary fellow of the American Institute of Architects (AIA)
2012	Royal Gold Medal des Royal Institute of British Architects	Receives the Gold Medal of the Royal Institute of British Architects
2013	Ehrenmitgliedschaft der Architectural Association, London	Becomes an honorary member of the Architectural Association, London

Impressum/Imprint

Herausgeber/Editor:
Klaus Kinold-Stiftung Architektur + Fotografie,
München/Munich

Text/Texts:
Wolfgang Jean Stock

Gestaltung/Design:
Klaus Kinold, Dagmar Zacher

Übersetzung/Translations:
Russell Stockman

Korrektorat Englisch/Proofreading English:
David Sánchez

Lithographie/Separations:
Serum Network GmbH, München/Munich

Druck und Bindung/Printing and binding:
Gotteswinter und Fibo Druck und Verlags GmbH,
München/Munich

Printed in Germany

© 2025 Hirmer Verlag GmbH, München/Munich
© Fotografien: Klaus Kinold, München/Munich
© Text: Wolfgang Jean Stock, München/Munich

Frontispiz/Frontispiece:
Verwaltungsgebäude/Headquarters Centraal Beheer,
Apeldoorn, 1990

Die deutsche Nationalbibliothek verzeichnet diese Publikation in der Deutschen Nationalbibliografie; detaillierte bibliografische Angaben sind im Internet über http://dnb.de abrufbar/ The Deutsche Nationalbibliothek holds a record of this publication in the Deutsche Nationalbibliografie; detailed bibliographical data can be found at http://dnb.de

ISBN 978-3-7774-3662-3

Hirmer Verlag
Bayerstraße 57-59
80335 München

www.hirmerverlag.de
www.hirmerpublishers.com